ON

THE THEORY AND PRACTICE

OF

WATER-MEADOWS.

By Ph. PUSEY, M.P.

LONDON.

MDCCCXLIX.

FROM THE

JOURNAL OF THE ROYAL AGRICULTURAL SOCIETY OF ENGLAND,

VOL. X., PART II.

THEORY AND PRACTICE

WATER-MEADOWS.

A FEW years since some slight account of Devonshire water-meadows, and of the cheap rate at which they are formed, was inserted by me in this Journal. Having now formed some myself on the same plan in Berkshire, I am thus enabled to state distinctly what they have cost me; and if the money so spent yield a profit of 30 per cent., which at a moderate estimate it can be shown to do, this mode of improvement must deserve the attention of landlords, now especially, when tenants stand so much in need of assistance, and labourers of employment.

It is well known that, in forming water-meadows, to moisten them is not the main object, the stream being laid on chiefly in winter, when commonly the ground is already rather too wet. Yet a slight film of water trickling then over the surface, for it must not stagnate, rouses the sleeping grass, tinges it with living green amidst snows or frost, and brings forth a luxuriant crop in early spring, just when it is most wanted, while the other meadows are still bare and brown. It is a cheerful sight to see the wild birds haunting these green spots among the hoar-frost at Christmas; or the lambs, with their mothers, folded on them in March. A water-meadow is the triumph of agricultural art, changing, as it does, the very seasons: but though our rustic forefathers so long since mastered the result, the mode of the water's action has been left a mystery. It consists not in moistening the roots, for they are moist enough—nor yet in covering the surface, for *stagnant* surface-water is merely injurious, the fluid must be kept in motion, however slow—it is not in the deposit of fine mud, for though the first runnings after the autumn rains are rendered the most beneficial by the thickness of the waters, a stream, clear as crystal, is often employed. About Exmoor I have

B 2

seen a stream issuing near the top of a steep moor-side, down which. in its descent, it draws a straight line of vivid verdure, visible at a mile's distance against the black heath. Not but where a deposit does take place, it is most beneficial. However dull the stream when it enters, after trickling through the grass it issues clear. So that, as I have heard, at Tempsford, a sluggish mill-stream previously thick, allows you, after it has passed over the meadows, to detect the pike basking six feet deep under its surface. The matter thus left behind is proved to be fertilizing by the superior efficacy of the first floods ; but where are we to seek the cause of the *clear* water's action ? An experienced maker of water-meadows examining a spring, told me, after feeling the water by holding some of it in the palm of his hand, that it must be good for watering : all streams, it should be remembered, are not equally good, some are even injurious. When asked the ground of his opinion, he answered, that it felt warm and oily. To confine ourselves for the present to the former quality warmth—springs, issuing as they do from different depths, and partaking therefore more or less largely of the earth's central heat, vary much in their temperature, though most of them, perhaps all, are warmer than the earth's surface in winter. But the warmer the spring the better it is considered for water-meadows in Devonshire, where springs are much used for the purpose; elsewhere it is chiefly small rivers which are so employed. We must suppose, then, that the water acts in irrigation partly by the warmth it communicates to the soil. A curious proof of this view is afforded by the following circumstance :—There is a stream in Devonshire which was useless in irrigation until it reached a station of the Atmospheric Railway, where warm water escaping into it from the steam-engine, rendered it *at that point, for the first time, beneficial to the land it passed over.* In that county where the warmth of springs is much studied on this very account, a wide difference of temperature is found in springs issuing from the same hill-side. Some springs freeze at once in a hard frost, a thick basin of ice forming around the well-head. Another spring a few hundred yards off may be seen on a frosty morning steaming like a cauldron. It not only does not freeze at the source, but its waters will continue to pass in a fluid state over meadows during a frost. The warm spring is selected for irrigation : the cold one is kept aloof. It is also supposed that the south sides of hills yield warmer streams than the north sides, and these southern streams are therefore preferred for meadows. We may safely conclude then, I think, though I have never seen it so stated in any agricultural work,*

---

* Since the above was written I find that, though recent agricultural works deny the efficacy of warmth in irrigation, Sir H. Davy, himself a west-countryman, asserts it in his Agricultural Chemistry.

that the main principle of irrigation is the warmth produced by the water trickling over the surface. Warmth is a prime agent in vegetation, and a slight difference in warmth has a marked effect in hastening or retarding the growth of plants. On hills of a very moderate height—as the chalk range in Berkshire—the harvest is sometimes a fortnight later than in the vale at their feet. The warmth of the London air opens the buds earlier. A southern wall, by reflecting heat, hastens the growth of vegetables near its foot. The warm spring too or river does not merely flow over the surface, but sinks largely into the land if it be at all porous, and *such* land is *most* benefited by irrigation ; some of the best water-meadows being mere gravels, almost bare of soil. Thus the roots of the grass are kept in a state of genial warmth. But the conclusive argument, as appears to me, may be drawn from a very curious operation called Gurneyism, of which an account was given in the seventh volume of this Journal.

Mr. Gurney having observed, what many may have remarked, that wherever any loose object, a bare branch, or an old gate, lies on a meadow in March, the grass grows exuberantly beneath it, conceived the idea of spreading a field with straw, at the rate of about a ton to the acre, and thus promoting the growth of the grass. The scheme succeeded so well that it was adopted by many neighbouring farmers in Cornwall ; and thus, curiously enough, a thin coat of dry straw produced the same effect which had hitherto been obtained only by a thin sheet of moving water. How, it may be asked, did the straw produce its effect? I can see but one way. Gardeners, it is well known, spread light nets over their young crops in order to protect them from morning frosts in the spring. This effect is clearly due to the interception of the radiation of heat. The earth is constantly sending forth, in a perpendicular direction upwards into empty space, especially when the sky is clear, its warmth derived from the sun, just as a stove darts its heat around it ; but a very slight interruption, such as the gardener's net, is found to check the passage of the heat, and thus to prevent that morning frost on the surface so much dreaded by gardeners. Gurneyism must act in a like manner, though on a larger scale, by preventing the escape of the natural warmth from the soil of a meadow. Irrigation, we have had reason to conclude, acts by imparting to the meadow the superior warmth of the stream or the spring. The effect is the same : the mode of action is the same nearly. The difference is as between covering up a sick man with blankets, or placing him in a warm bath. The one is stronger treatment than the other, and so also irrigation acts in winter—Gurneyism only in spring. It may even be questioned, I think, whether irrigation do not also act in some degree by intercepting the radiation of heat. Mr. Gurney found that *round rods of transparent glass* suspended over grass acted as well as opaque bodies in promoting its growth. Is it not possible that the rippling water may act like these rods of glass? It is true that water, after passing over a portion of water-meadow, is found to have lost much of its power when turned over another portion. This we should expect, because in travelling over and through the ground it has parted with its native heat, and will produce a diminished effect. I believe that it produces still some effect, otherwise the conjecture must, of course, fall to the ground —the point need, however, not be pursued further.

But, it may be asked, if streams act by their warmth when turned over meadows, why do not all streams of the same temperature act equally well? Why are some streams better than others? Why do some not act at all? The answer, I believe, is this. Several foreign substances, present sometimes in streams, are found by experience to be noxious to vegetation. Thus it was mentioned above that water for irrigation should feel, in a practised hand, oily as well as warm. This oiliness, I suppose, is the same with what is commonly called softness, the opposite of hardness, which is caused by the presence of carbonic acid, of which latter quality the laundress also complains when the soap will not dissolve in her washing-tub without the aid of wood ashes or of soda. A spring which contains carbonic acid largely is a petrifying one. We have some streamlets in this neighbourhood which, for the first mile or two of their course, encrust their sides and bottoms with lime. Such are declared to be unfit for irrigation, why I know not, but so experience teaches. It is observed that the two favourable and the two unfavourable qualities are generally found together in springs; softness with warmth, and cold with hardness. Ochrey springs, having on their surface a film, which presents the colours of the rainbow, and containing iron, are said also to be injurious; though in one district this iridescence was mentioned to me as even a favourable sign for irrigation. There is another substance most certainly mischievous to vegetation—the matter suspended in bog-water. Such water is destructive to the growth of meadow-grass. Marsh peat is itself so highly injurious, that when marsh peat has been put by a mistake into flower-beds for the growth of rhododendrons, it destroyed the garden turf for some breadth on each border. But this is not a hopeless obstacle, though found in a stream. I have seen water which a year or two before dribbling from a bog had been worse than useless, now issuing from the drain-pipes of that bog, *itself* cultivated, and, after resting in a reservoir, spreading verdure over a field lower down the hill-side. This vegetable extract, however, sometimes infects rivers themselves, as in the romantic scenery of West Somerset round Dulverton, a neighbourhood well known to fishermen. In that beau-

tiful district, four mountain torrents, rushing in a perpetual fall
along deep wooded valleys, join to form the river on which Exeter
stands. The Haddyo has the finest trout, and is best for water-
meadows. The Exe is moderate in both respects. The Barle
has poor trout, and is useless, or if not utterly useless, is rated
so low that other streams are carried over it by wooden aqueducts
for irrigating the fields on its very banks. The Danesbrook has
no trout, and is injurious upon meadows. The Barle and the
Danesbrook,* though clear as crystal, are brown as a cairngorm
with bog-water from Exmoor. When those moors are drained,
the fish may yet thrive in their waters, and the winter's grass
become green on their banks. It may be instructive to pursue
the united streams further. The conjoint river is unfit for watering until it has received another stream of excellent quality near

---

* I shall be forgiven for recalling to the reader that these romantic
streams have twice been admitted into English poetry—once by the late
Dean of Manchester :—

> " Oh, how I love the woody steeps to climb
> Which overhang thy solitary stream,
> Clear-flowing Barle ! or tread the broken stones
> Round which thy never-ceasing waters foam,
> And ever and anon rough-tumbling roar
> Beneath the oaken shade. . . . . .
> And thou, romantic spot where close beneath
> Mountsey's proud brow and Anstey's stately moor
> Danesbrook and Barle their noisy streams unite :
> Upon your sides abrupt the pausing eye
> Dwells charmed as it views each sparkling spring
> Shine through the gloomy woods and trickle down."
>
> *Miscellaneous Poetry, by Hon. and Rev. W. Herbert,* 1801.

And once again, among a later generation, in the tender recollections
of his boyhood, by a dear departed friend :—

> " With beating heart how many a reckless day
> Has marked my boyish step delighted bend
> Where Haddon's heights of purple heath ascend,
> Where Hawkridge' wild and sullen wastes extend :
> And verdant Storridge to the thundering wave
> His mighty mass of oaken forest gave
> By Haddyo's foaming flood and Danesbrook's tide
> That parted once a rival people's pride. . . . . .
> Here have I heard in summer's liveliest glow
> Mid hail and mist the raging tempest blow,
> Eternally on hoarse resounding shore
> The infant Exe with tide impetuous roar.
>
> .   .   .   .   .   .
>
> In Pixton's woods the chase was fierce and strong ;
> At night their limbs on couch of heather spread,
> The mountain fern wild pillow for their head,
> And, if they listed melody, might hear
> Our rushing Barle make music for their ear."
>
> *The Moor, by the late Earl of Carnarvon.*

—PH. PUSEY.

to Bampton, after which it is capable of being used not alone, indeed yet, but to assist in making up the volume of tributary streams which are diverted along its banks. When the Exe however, now a broad river, has passed through the busy town of Tiverton—every street of which has a running stream washing away the ordure—the Exe becomes again fertilizing, and meadows are formed to receive its waters. The theory of irrigation appears then to be this :—Water acts upon meadows by imparting its warmth to them; perhaps also as a covering, by enabling them to retain their own warmth. If the water contain mud or fine soil its action is stronger. If the drainings of yards or of towns, stronger still. On the other hand, the colder the stream the less likely it is to act, and its powers are weakened or destroyed by the presence of carbonic acid (by hardness), or of iron, or of bog-water. The quality of the fish has been seen to indicate that of the water. A spring haunted by woodcocks will be good for water-meadows.. The bird finds the ground about these warmer springs softer for his searching bill. A well-known herb, the *watercress*, is said to be an *unfailing* witness for the goodness of the stream along whose bottom it flourishes.

We may now turn from the theory to the practice of irrigation. Water-meadows are formed on two systems. In the southern counties, Hampshire, Berks, Wilts, Gloucester, and Dorset, the Itchin, the Kennet, the Avon, and other rivers, are diverted; and the neighbouring land being flat is entirely reshaped to receive them. The turf is pared. The whole surface is laid up in high regular ridges, about thirty feet wide, along whose summit the water runs in gutters, overflowing the sides to the bottom, where other gutters receive them and carry them off. In form the meadows are like the sea after a storm, when the long waves are subsiding.

Plan of Water-Meadow.

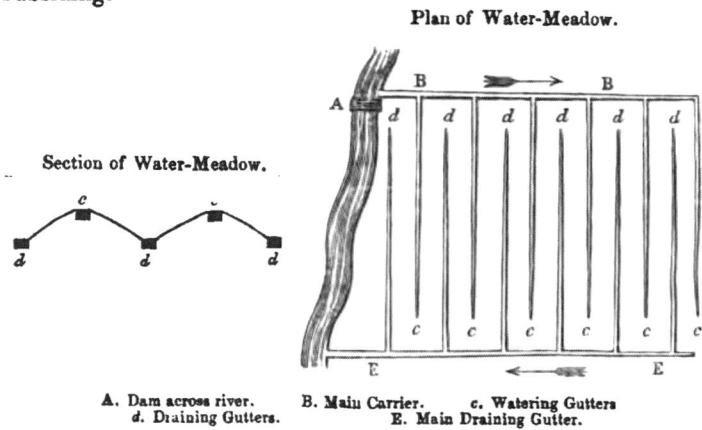

Section of Water-Meadow.

A. Dam across river.　　B. Main Carrier.　　c. Watering Gutters
d. Draining Gutters.　　　　E. Main Draining Gutter.

Those who are conversant with earth-works will see at once that to make a water-meadow on this plan must be an expensive process. Twenty pounds per acre would be a low average: thirty pounds not unusual. I remember having asked in Dorsetshire to see a cheap water-meadow, and being shown a field of eight or ten acres, which had just been made *at a cost of forty-five pounds for each acre.* Few new water-meadows, however, are any longer made in these southern counties, as the heavy expense of the system is barely compensated, now that the growth of green crops has supplied more food for flocks in March and April. It is to the south-west we must turn, to Somerset and to Devonshire, for patterns of future irrigation. In those two lovely counties, which have the valleys without the Alps of Switzerland, abundant streams roll cheerfully in a rapid descent over stones, or among mossy rocks, and the sheltered sides shelving rapidly upwards, have long since tempted the farmers to lead the water along their sloping face in tiers of channels, each of which receiving the overflow from above, as it begins to gather irregularly, receives it in a level trough to brim over anew, until it reaches the lowest channel, which delivers it back to the river's bed. The horseman as he rides along sees meadows of a few acres rising above his head, bright as emerald, glistening against the sun with their thin film of water, alternating with orchards in which cottages are nestled, that seem to cling to the hill, with a canopy of oak copse above, whose russet leaves, a remnant of the last summer, look the ruddier against the narrow space of blue sky that roofs in the glen. These are called catch-meadows, because each trench thus catches the water from its neighbour above it.

Section of Lower Part of a Valley.

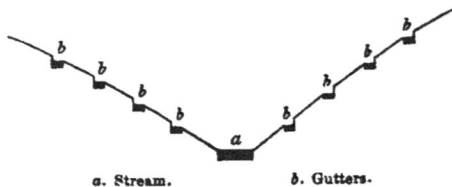

a. Stream.   b. Gutters.

The catch-meadow is as cheap as the water-meadow is expensive to form. For the slope being already there, it is necessary but to take the levels for the gutters; which being done, these may be dug, and the surface be laid smooth, for two or three pounds per acre instead of twenty or thirty. I have seen near Winsford, a water-meadow on the hang of a hill so steep that one could scarcely climb it without help of the hands. It had been until lately rough furze ground. The tenant had given it rent free to a labourer for two years. The labourer broke it up, grew two crops of potatoes for himself, smoothed it, and actually cut the gutters, so that the farmer had converted moorland into rich grass at the cost only of a good dressing of lime which was given it. Many a hill-side in Cardiganshire, or Argyleshire, or Kerry, might be thus transmuted, if one energetic landowner would lead the way. Catch-meadows have been successfully formed in more level counties by the Duke of Portland, and by Lord Hatherton, who possessed natural slopes. But most English streams are sluggish, flowing through level tracts. It is distinctly stated in one of our best and handiest agricultural works, "The Dictionary of the Farm," by the late Mr. Rham, that "catchwork is only applicable where there is a considerable fall of water, and a gentle declivity towards the river." If this prevailing opinion be sound, a large part of England must remain without increase of its irrigation.

This opinion, however, is a mistake; for in Devonshire—the classic land of catch-meadows—catchwork has been lately applied to levels as flat as the banks of the Cherwell, and is spreading rapidly on such levels. At Killerton, near Exeter, Sir Thomas Acland has two wide catch-meadows, each of about 60 acres, without perceptible fall, called 'Wish meadows' and 'Beer-marshes' (in Devonshire a meadow means a water-meadow; a low unwatered grass-field is called a marsh), and Lord Polimore, on a farm occupied by Mr. Norris, has a catch-meadow 3 furlongs long, with a fall in that distance of *only four inches and a half*; what is important, the land is irrigated in the line of this fall, that is, by cross gutters. For there are two falls we have to consider in catchwork, as in the quotation from Mr. Rham, the fall of the stream *onwards* and the fall of the land towards the stream *sideways*. The fall of the stream is required for diverting its water to a point from which it may run over the land: the fall of the land is required for carrying the water off from the land into a lower part of the stream. A stream might have but a slight fall, say a foot, in passing through a water-meadow a quarter of a mile long, yet if the neighbouring land shelved towards the stream, and if the meadow were but 200 yards broad with the stream in the middle, there would be a side fall for the water returning over the land into the stream equal to 1 foot in 300, though the fall of the river is assumed to be only 1 foot in 1320.

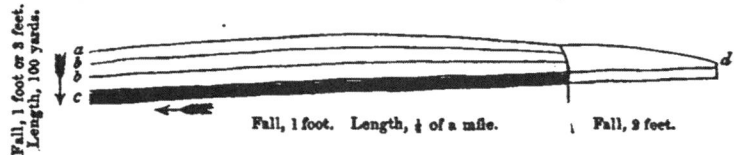

f a little higher up there were a fall of 2 feet, and the water could there be diverted, a *side* fall of 3 feet, or of 1 in 100, might be obtained on the water-meadow.

But if the land adjoining a stream do not shelve sideways, the only fall to be obtained will be in the direction of the river's descent, and that fall cannot be increased by damming the stream higher up. The gutters must be cut athwart the line of the river, and the course of the irrigating water must be in the same direction with the course of the stream thus,—

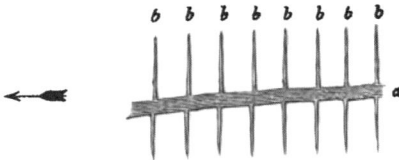

a. River. *b.* Watering gutters.

In this case it follows that the fall of the irrigated land cannot exceed the fall of the river. Since the fall of the river on this meadow of Lord Poltimore's is only 4½ inches in a course of 3 furlongs, or 1980 feet, and the course of irrigation is not lateral but direct, it follows that the fall of irrigation is but 1 in 5280. This is so wonderfully low, that unless the measurement had been given me by the person who laid it out I could not have believed it, for the fall considered desirable, if not necessary, on the old-fashioned system is about 1 in 18. A new meadow is now being made for Lord Poltimore where the river has a fall of 2½ feet only in half a mile length. On one side of the stream the field is 2 furlongs wide, so that even where the fall is lateral it will be but 2½ in 2 furlongs, or 1 in 528. Another is being made for Mr. Barber with the exceedingly low fall of 2½ inches in 2½ furlongs. This is a direct irrigation. The fall of *one inch in a furlong*, or 1 in 7920, is remarkable even according to the new system of Devonshire. There is indeed one *old* meadow near Crediton exceedingly flat, so flat that, as the stream which waters it brings down large quantities of mould from the hills, as well as refuse from the town, the land rises rapidly, and in order to keep down the levels the surface has been removed twice in seven years to a depth of 2 feet, to be carted off as a top-dressing for other fields. These flat meadows are now spreading widely in South Devon. That they pay for their formation there can be no doubt, costing from three to four pounds an acre to form, and yielding three pounds of rent, whereof two pounds may be taken as the new value imparted by the operation. This, for an average rate of profit, is a very high one. In single cases it is exceeded. About two miles from Exeter there is a small property of 156 acres, all but eight of which, that are orchard-ground, are watered by two moderate brooks. *It is let at more than six pounds an acre all round* to different occupiers. Three acres, worth naturally three pounds an acre, let at *ten* pounds, six acres at eight pounds per acre. The whole was worth about two pounds an acre originally, and the portion recently made cost about three pounds twelve shillings per acre to form. These are actual *lettings*. The Clipstone water-meadows are *valued* by Mr. Denison at eleven pounds fourteen shillings per acre yearly, without allowance for rates and taxes. They are, indeed, a noble creation of the Duke of Portland's. Great difficulties have been overcome, and great perfection attained. As you wind up the valley you see nothing but one universal luxuriant tapestry of grass spread on each side along the well-moulded slopes—

" Hic ver assiduum atque *alienis* mensibus æstas."

" The fields here Spring's perpetual beauties crown,
    Here Summer shines in seasons not her own." *

This work, however, cost his Grace *one hundred and thirty pounds* per acre in forming, or 39,297*l.* for 300 acres—a price few could afford. In the above case from the neighbourhood of Exeter, we have the value not merely estimated, but realized in the form of rent, and the cost insignificant. If I dwell often on cheapness of construction in farming it is because no improvement can become general if it be not also cheap. It is by reducing the cost of production that the Lancashire manufacturers have sent our cottons round the whole world.

As to the management of the catch-meadows in Devonshire, the watering is begun in autumn with the heavy rains, and great importance is attached to these first floodings. Sometimes the use of a stream is divided among neighbouring farmers by periods of three days. I have been told by one who contracts to keep such meadows in order, that when an unneighbourly farmer insists on keeping his water for the full term, that is till midnight, my informant is obliged to remain out half the night, perhaps wet to his skin, setting the bays and distributing the water on the land of the next recipient, who, he says, might lose ten shillings an acre if he waited till morning. So much value does the experience of Devonshire attach to water.

Sometimes a crop of feed is forced before Christmas; but in general the water is so shifted, that the strength of the land and the grass may be reserved for an early crop, which in Devonshire is often ready by the end of February. If the ewes are admitted into a field on the 1st of March, they feed it down perhaps in a fortnight, and are removed. The water is let in, and kept on

---

* Warton's Virgil.

for a fortnight; after a few days there is a good bite of grass, and the ewes are let in once more. Sometimes on good land, and in good seasons, a third crop even of feed is grown before the land is laid up for hay, which is generally done on the 1st of May; in six weeks from that time, by the middle of June, the hay is ready to cut. Afterwards the meadow is "damped," that is, watered for about three days. A longer watering is improper in warm weather, as it leaves a white scum on the land, the dried remains of the same loose green vegetable matter (a *conferva*), which is often seen in stagnant ditches.

Such being the cheapness and such the advantages of the *level* catch-meadow in Devonshire, it becomes an important question whether the system would answer generally in the south of England. A *question* it is certainly, for the marked difference of climate forbids us to form a peremptory conclusion.

It is well known now, that the western sides of both England and Ireland are more favourable to grass than the eastern sides; the western breezes being loaded with vapour which, whether retained in its invisible form or condensed as rain, is most propitious to vegetation. The air too is warmer in winter, and, the sky being more clouded, the sun less scorching in summer. On a naked field it is as difficult to check the natural grasses in Devonshire as to bring a turf, if wanted, in Berkshire. Severe frosts too are much less frequent in Devonshire, as well in winter as spring, at which latter period they destroy grass which has been forced forwards, unless its roots be well covered with running water. Two years since, however, I determined to try the experiment in Berkshire, and secured the assistance of an experienced "gutterer" (as the makers of water-meadows are called in Devonshire), Mr. Ley, of Newton St. Cyr, near Exeter, who with his son had laid out the meadows instanced above for their exceedingly low gradients—a matter of the nicest skill in agricultural engineering. His son formed for me sixty acres, at a contract price of 4*l.* per acre, to which price must be added 30*s.* an acre for bringing water from the streams, and for trunks and sluices. Much of this land is flat, and there is also a great scarcity of water. Catchwork, it should be remarked, has the further advantage, that it works not only with little *fall*, but with little *water*, as upon fields almost level the water with so slight a fall flows very slowly. The water is also spread very *thinly*. Mr. Ley says that, if a catch-meadow be laid out well, you ought to be able to walk across it, while the water is on, without wetting your feet. This perhaps is a figure of speech, but it illustrates the point. The meadows were completed early in 1848; but appeared, excepting one small field, to be *a total failure*. The crop was not earlier than in other years. Mr. J. Ley accounted for the deficiency by the natural poverty of the soil, and its want of condition. Both these imputations were just; but the undertaking seemed hopeless enough. I dwell upon the circumstance, because it may be useful to others. It seems to be a principle that irrigation may gradually raise the condition of land, but requires either good land or fair condition to produce a marked immediate effect. One field looked decidedly worse than before, because there had been previously more moss than grass on it, and the moss had been killed by the water. But on the worst part of that field the ashes of some burnt bull-peats or hassock-grass had been spread, and a luxuriant crop of grass had sprung up. The hint was taken, and there being peat at command for burning, a liberal dose of ashes was applied in March, 1849. The effect was marvellous, especially on some worn out rye-grass, which is now full of young clover and is become at once a *close sward*. This is not the case where *either* the ashes or the water have been deficient. Here is a remarkable agreement with what is said of Gurneyism in the following passage:*—

"Many experiments were made. The results of those experiments were very interesting. They showed that the action was general; that the difference in growth in a given time was *in proportion* to the natural *fertility* of the soil. On some of the coarse moors where experiments were tried, the increase of growth was very slow as compared to better soils. It was found that the rate of action was also influenced by *artificial manuring*, and that the increase of vegetation was in a *ratio* with the natural quantity that would be produced by a given manure when laid on a field, and not assisted by the operation of any fibrous covering. A certain quantity of stall-dung, which would *double* the quantity of grass in a given time when laid on in the usual way, was found to increase it to *six* times when properly treated with fibrous covering."

It appears to me that in irrigation also the water does not merely add to the produce, but tends to double or treble it. If the produce by other means be half a ton, water will make it one ton. If the produce be one ton, it will become two tons by irrigation; a remarkable agreement with the action of fibrous covering, and a great encouragement to maintain or to raise the condition of water-meadows.

In one way or other, partly by ashing the land, partly by the irrigation alone, an entire change was made by last spring. The grass grew so rapidly that we could not feed it all off, and were obliged unwillingly to make much of it into hay. I say unwillingly, because to carry off a crop of hay is of course not the way to raise the condition of the land. As far as possible, however, sheep were penned regularly over the new catch-meadows, in general three times successively on the same land, and partly with artificial food because they were new and poor; but to show

---

* Journal of Royal Agricultural Society, Vol. vii. p. 279.

the amount of stock kept, I will give the account of sheep folded on a small field without other food. The field is under two acres, better land than the rest, but so much out of condition that latterly the hay-crop had been hardly worth cutting.

	Day's keep of a Sheep.
First penning, sheep put on, but grass too strong to feed, and made into hay, say only · · · · ·	3,000
Second feeding, 400 lambs for eight days, say 240 sheep · ·	1,920
Third penning, 250 sheep for ten days · · · · ·	2,500
Fourth ditto, 250 sheep, fourteen days · · · · ·	3,500
	10,920

The total amounts to 5 months' keep for 73 sheep on two acres, *thirty-six* sheep to an acre.

The calculation is made for five months, because that is the period for which the wintering of sheep on turnips is reckoned. A thoroughly good crop of turnips is said in Lincolnshire to keep *ten* sheep an acre for five months. It is difficult to find a standard of comparison upon grass-land, because beasts and sheep are usually grazed together. I know one instance, however, in which sheep were fattened on grass-land in the five summer months at the rate of *seven* sheep to an acre, and the number was thought to be large. This might be equal, however, to *fourteen* sheep of mine, which were merely kept in store order. Still the account would stand thus: *fourteen* sheep kept on an acre of superior grazing land unwatered, *thirty-six* sheep on an acre of moderate land watered. The very high rate of my sheep to the acre certainly surprises me, but the figures are perfectly accurate. The large number may be partly accounted for by a peculiarity of the management, namely, that the sheep were folded not only for the first time, but every time after, instead of roaming at large. In his report upon Gloucestershire, Mr. Bravender mentions that a farmer who adopted this system found an increase of twenty per cent. in the number of sheep he could keep on his farm. This point seems to deserve attention, *independently* of irrigation. The allowance of 20 per cent. for folding would still leave the numbers at 14 and 29. But as sheep at turnips are equally folded, the comparative numbers per acre will there stand at *thirty-six* and at *ten*, not to mention the expense of cultivation for turnips, and the absence of labour on water-meadows once formed. This meadow is a very flat one; in fact before it was levelled it appeared to have no fall; there is a fall however of 3 feet 8 inches in 140 yards, or 1 in 114. I mention this because the most doubtful point for our cold counties seems to me to be the slow fall, and hitherto certainly a fall six times sharper, has been thought requisite. On other parts of my new meadows a much lower fall is found sufficient.

As in other branches of farming, so in the management of water-meadows, constant attention and the master's eye are essential to complete success. Even in Devonshire, where all understand water-meadows, the farmer's management materially affects their production. The plan of repeated folding has answered, as has been seen, with me hitherto. On many water-meadows, where the animals roam at large, they neglect to eat portions of the field which thus become rank. Besides, the droppings are distributed more equally. One agricultural work intimates that there is danger of rot in feeding sheep on water-meadows during summer. In Devonshire, I am told, they have no such fear, nor have I suffered by it as yet; but I gave my sheep large lumps of rock salt to lick constantly in their folds. The danger may arise from *improper* flooding in summer, or it may be a real risk, and I therefore mention it. It certainly occurred on a part of the Clipstone meadows. In new water-meadows which require to be raised in condition, I should particularly recommend it as a cheap way of effecting that object. Probably, if continued in after years, it might raise the condition to too high a point; in order to lower which it might be necessary that a crop of hay should be severed and carried off in the usual manner. The yield of food for sheep would be, of course, the same, though in a different form. I should also recommend folding when ashes are applied to the land: as ashes being what was called formerly a stimulant, a manure of quick but passing action, might impoverish the land if the sudden crop produced by them were carried off. If the grass be fed off on the land, the extra produce is returned to it, and a solid foundation of future high condition is laid.

There is another point of detail which appears to answer. In folding the sheep I endeavour to have the hurdles so set that on each day, or second day, as they are shifted forwards, the water may be passed over the recently manured land. Every one knows the strong smell of a sheep-fold. Without entering upon the power of water to fix ammonia, a substance on which it is dangerous unless for a chemist to enter, and which led even Liebig astray, there is no doubt that the water thus following destroys the stench and must therefore distribute the manure. In fact, when this is carefully done no spots of dark herbage are seen to arise from the droppings. The water carries the salts *down* among the roots of the plants: for a great deal of the water sinks *into* the earth. When land is formed into water-meadow it is rather disheartening for a beginner to see a strong stream sink for days into the bottom of the carrier without overflowing at all; and when it does at last overflow, to see it creep over the land, advancing but a few inches perhaps in an hour. Even though the stream be strong it sinks through the worm-holes, from which the escape of the air-bubbles produces a general noise like the distant singing of birds ; the ground indeed is said to *sing*.   The worms however die (they are found dead in large numbers), and the pores of the earth are gradually filled up by fine particles of soil carried down by the water.   It is a good sign when the water begins to lie in the bottom of the gutters after the stream is drawn off.   This effect may be anticipated by rendering the water muddy where that is possible, or, according to Mr. Roales in his Prize Essay, by spreading fine earth on the surface.

Still a great deal of water is drunk by the land, and this circumstance may be made serviceable.   In summer only "damping," as it is called, is allowable.   Here, however, in a dry summer we have not water enough even for damping.   But by leaving the gutters brimfull, so that the whole stream might be absorbed in the channels, I was enabled to make the most of the dribbling brook which the long drought had left, and to keep some very dry land green and grassy, while other pastures were parched and had ceased growing.   For our inland counties, which are subject in summer to constant droughts, I believe that this power of keeping the land moist would *alone go far to pay the cost of making a catch-meadow.*

There is another use which may be made of water-meadows. The two streams employed here I have turned through two of the farm-yards.   The cattle in these yards are kept loose, even while fattening, in the old-fashioned way, though tied up at feeding-time.   When heavy rains come, the muck-water is washed down into the passing stream, and distributed over the meadow without labour to man or to horse.   In this case, and whenever a reservoir is filled with black water from other yards, as happens in sudden rains, the manager is desired to put only so much of this rich water on a piece of the ground as will sink into it, and then to turn the dark liquor over a fresh portion of meadow.   This is done lest the soluble salts should be carried away over the surface of the field into the stream, and so wasted.   As to the winter management of the water it may generally be left on any particular portion for a fortnight at once.   When the grass turns dark, the water should be taken off.   A standard Scotch work on farming directs that it should be taken off on the arrival of frost. The true rule, however, at least in Devonshire, is not to *take it off* nor to *lay it on* in a frost ;—not to take it off, because the water freezing on the ground forms a coat of ice which protects the grass exactly as a covering of snow guards the young wheat,—not to lay it on, because the ground, being already frozen, can be no longer protected.

There is a novel use of irrigation which I may be permitted to

c

mention, as it has answered in the only experiment I have hitherto made—the application, I mean, of artificial manures. The two chosen were—guano, as an universal manure; and sulphate of ammonia, the refuse, I believe, of gas-works, as being the most likely of chemical salts to favour the growth of grass. The guano was applied by mixing it in the gutter as the water was laid on; the ammonia by distributing it along the edge of the same gutter in another part, where it was rapidly dissolved by the water. Both applications have succeeded: the *chemical salt* answered the *best*. The land should be previously dry, that the solution may enter it.

It may now be convenient, perhaps, to sum up shortly some of the practical points mentioned above.

It is clear that in the moist climate of Devonshire the system of catchwork which originated on steep slopes has been gradually transferred to land which an unpractised eye would regard as a dead flat.

It appears also that this inexpensive method of irrigation may be transferred in *some* degree to our drier and colder inland counties, though caution is still necessary, as Mr. Denison says, that at Clipstone Park, 1 in 9 is the best fall, and that very flat lands *will* not answer for irrigation. Clipstone Park, however, is far towards the north. The degree of fall suited for each shade of climate is matter for further trial. It should be observed, that since the Devonshire system does not profess to recast the land on a perfect model, but only to effect its object by using and improving the natural irregularities of the surface, the distribution of the water on the level catch-meadows will not be perfect at first; but a constant improvement may be made in these meadows by rolling them while they are wet, and by using the earth which is taken out of the gutters in cleansing them every autumn, for raising gradually any spots where the water lodges.

It should also be remembered that land, if at all unsound, must be underdrained when it is irrigated, and the drains must be larger than ordinary, as Mr. Denison informs us in the excellent paper* to which reference has already been made. The drains should be laid so that the water issuing from them may be made to flow again over on a lower part of the meadow. Drains are the only source of water on Lord Hatherton's meadows at Teddesley.

The safest mode of agricultural improvement is, not the adoption of entirely new principles or contrivances, but the cautious yet courageous development of existing practice. The level catch-meadow is clearly a promising ground to be worked out; and in

* See Journal, vol. i.

endeavouring to carry it further, the following points should, I think, be attended to :—

1. The increased use of folding for sheep.
2. The conveyance of the stream through farmyards, as the simplest method of preventing the waste of manure.
3. The rapid application of the water as the sheep-pens are shifted, for preventing the waste of manure deposited on the land.
4. The increased use of the water for maintaining vegetation during the droughts of summer.
5. The use of the water for diffusing chemical manures on the land watered.
6. The cultivation of Italian rye-grass, which grows three times as rapidly as the common meadow grasses under the influence of irrigation.
7. It being necessary, where the stream is scanty, to form a reservoir, the ornamental sheets of parks may be used for the purpose, by placing, as I have done, an additional but removable board on the sluice-gate, so as to raise the pond occasionally a few inches above its level —a considerable rise for the purpose, if the sheet of water be at all extensive.

There is nothing more that I need now add. I will not pretend to teach how catch-meadows are to be made. Since the natural irregularities of the ground, which an unpractised eye would overlook, are to be used for distributing the water, the work must be left to a professional manager, as in Devonshire. Even among "gutterers" there is great difference of skill; thus it is said of Mr. Ley, that his eye is better than many another man's level. I have proved what I set out by promising, that money expended on catch-meadows may pay 30 or even 50 per cent.; and as the work is done by contract, there can be no error as to its cost. In any branch of manufacture, to prove this fact would be to ensure its immediate accomplishment. If such a profit were likely to arise from cutting through the Isthmus of Suez or Panama the canals would be dug at once. Much more persuasion I know is needed in stimulating landlords to the improvement of even English estates. I will only say that it is mainly these catch-meadows which enable me to keep a flock of 550 ewes, and winter their lambs also, on nearly the same farm upon which my predecessor kept 170 ewes with their lambs. There is one test, however, often applied by farmers, when a person adopts and recommends some improvement in farming. They ask the question,—Has he gone on with it? This is a very good test, for there are many disappointments in new systems of farming. I may therefore be allowed to mention, that having last year suspended any fresh plan of irrigation, on account of the apparent failure of those which were already executed, I have contracted this winter for 26 acres of catch-meadow to be made at 3*l.* 10*s.*, and 30 more at only 2*l.* an acre. But what is described gives no clear impression; a work of art must be seen. Next year, however, our Society meets at Exeter. July, indeed, is not a good season for seeing catch-meadows, as the water is not upon them, and the grass wears no unusual verdure. Still the method of irrigation may be even then understood, and some one of the meadows could easily be watered slightly for the inspection of visitors. To see what might be done in Wales or in Scotland, the owners of mountain properties might make a pleasant excursion along the Exe towards its source northwards. The scenery will beguile the way, and near the Bristol Channel they will find excellent samples of hill-side catch-meadows about Timberscombe and upon Dunkerry not much below the Beacon. For level meadows the patterns are to be found within ten miles of Exeter, and I hope that they will not be seen in vain by English gentlemen having villagers without winter work, as who of us is there that has not?

PUSEY, *Nov.* 23, 1849.

PRINTED BY W. CLOWES AND SONS, STAMFORD STREET.

CPSIA information can be obtained
at www.ICGtesting.com
Printed in the USA
LVRC011549140220
646991LV00004B/25